Whispered Prayers in the Arizona Desert:
The History of the Shrine of Santa Rita
2nd edition

Editorial Resources, Inc.

2020

ISBN 0-9745923-6-6

Preface

Exit ramp 279 off Interstate 10 in Southern Arizona seems no more significant than all the others, but on Vail Road, about a mile from the highway, just east of Tucson, Arizona, is a tiny Catholic church that has a story. The faded white adobe walls and the aging red tile roof attract no undue attention, and even during Mass on Saturday evenings and Sunday mornings there is no real commotion here. Most of the time, quiet surrounds the church nestled between the Southern Pacific railroad tracks, which once were such a vital link to civilization for the rural community of Vail, but now are so far less important. Vail's only church certainly is not a grand cathedral, but visitors stop by during the week sometimes, on their way to or from the tourist attractions of Colossal Cave and the Saguaro National Monument up the road. If you do find it, you probably live here or are lost, and either way, the church's story will not demand your notice. Nonetheless, Santa Rita was a gift to the Catholics of Vail, and gifts are special, so the story has become special as well.

In the local area so much has been written about the Shrine of Santa Rita in the Desert that much of the familiar tale takes on the tone of legend. Every few years, a newspaper article appears or a travel magazine recounts the anomalous tale of the Arizona desert shrine built in 1935 in memory of a Japanese doctor. Through the years, the details have varied widely: Dr. Jokichi Takamine has been credited with "discovering," "inventing," and "isolating" adrenaline, insulin, and penicillin. It becomes difficult to decide what to believe. Rumors surround the Shrine's story like a whispering mist; there's some connection to Cecil B. DeMille, and the cherry trees in Washington, DC, and the forests of New York, and the Emperor of Japan . . . the tale-bearing mist assures the listener. Various reports label Takamine as a prominent international figure instrumental in establishing peaceful relations between Japan and the United States, but also as a humble and retiring scientist ardently dedicated to his lonely pursuit of medical progress. He was a wealthy world-traveler who was recognized in prominent social circles, but was also a quiet paternal figure who championed the immigration of brilliant Japanese scientists to the United States early in the twentieth century.

Unfortunately, so little has been written recently about the Shrine and the Takamine family with reliable or identifiable sources, that the accounts become untrustworthy. Currently, interest is being renewed by several groups and individuals studying Takamine's historical accomplishments, so perhaps his story will be more widely known soon. For now though, separating fact from fiction in the Takamine history becomes difficult because the story is so interesting and romantic that any researcher would want all of the colorful facets of the tale to be true. The isolated chapel is romantic and does indeed have a fascinating history to impart, and that's why this story needs to be told and retold and kept alive. The union of two diverse cultures, Oriental and Occidental; the juncture of two distinct religions, Buddhism and Catholicism; and the marital alliance of a nineteenth-century Japanese physician and an American debutante all culminate in a rural chapel few people realize holds such a treasury of history. These converging opposites make this story extremely valuable. The Shrine of Santa Rita represents a part of our culture and a legacy of our forebears that threatens to vanish for want of our diligent attention. The facts need to be verified and the myths need to be investigated, so that all of us, but especially our children's children, will understand the importance of all the virtues that make up this anomaly in the desert: love, perseverance, faith, and diversity.

With the help of many other writers, I have made an attempt to ascertain the truth in this story. One intriguing resource is a hand-written manuscript in the files from the church rectory. This document is written by at least three separate writers who at various times attempted to record for posterity the stories of the Shrine, the Takamine family, Mrs. Caroline Takamine Beach, and Santa Rita. Each narrator obviously recognized the historical significance of the Shrine of Santa Rita, but only left this partial record of his or her search. Clues in the 40-page text suggest that one of the writers may have been Fr. William Gockel, a priest who served the mission of Santa Rita for over ten years at different times from 1948-1967. Parts of the document are transcribed passages from Dr. Takamine's 1928 biography, *Jokichi Takamine: A Record of His American Achievements*, by K. K. Kawakami. This book was family-approved and is understandably an encomium emphasizing only Dr. Takamine's many life accomplishments and ignoring the controversial issues that surround his fame and personal character.

The claim that somehow movie director Cecil B. DeMille financed the church becomes a much-diluted connection in reality. The link comes through the famous director's niece, Agnes. American dancer and choreographer Agnes de Mille's childhood memories of spending summers in Merriewold, New York, near the Takamine's elegant Japanese-styled estate during the early years of the twentieth century, which she recounts in *Where the Wings Grow* (1978), were most helpful in piecing together a patchwork story that certainly travelled far to finally settle into the heat and dust of the Arizona desert. De Mille's quasi-family relationship with Caroline Takamine offered her at least partial insight into a life of international prestige, wealth, and mystery.

Technically, Caroline Takamine was not related to Agnes de Mille, despite her designation by Agnes and her young cousins as "Aunt Caroline." Agnes's aunt, her mother Anna's sister-in-law, was Marie Hitch George, who in turn was sister to Caroline Hitch Takamine. The divergent sides of several families converged in the forests of New York state during the summers, and Agnes, a perceptive child, captured a glimpse of a life we can only dimly perceive despite the relatively short lapse of years between the beginning of this century and its rapidly-ascending close. De Mille briefly mentions the Shrine of Santa Rita in her memoir of life near the Takamine family, but goes into very little detail on the subsequent history of the church. After Caroline Takamine's first husband died in 1922, she married Vail rancher Charles P. Beach and won the admiration and gratitude of the community to which she donated the chapel.

Now, in 2020, the Shrine has existed for over 85 years as a spiritual foundation for the village of Vail and the surrounding rural countryside. The priests who have served the tiny chapel through the years have come quite literally from around the world. Many came to the dry heat of Arizona for their health; several died in Vail and are buried in Tucson; and many stopped only briefly at Santa Rita to serve her people and God and then moved on to other religious duties. All of them have contributed to the history of the Shrine of Santa Rita in the Desert. As recorded in 1996, Santa Rita first served as a mission outpost and later as a full-fledged parish with a resident priest, and not only has the Shrine joyfully celebrated many Holy Communions and 149 confirmations, 131 weddings, and 283 baptisms, but also Santa Rita has comforted parishioners during illnesses, emergencies, and funerals; 62 deaths were recorded in the official church record in 1996. Mrs. Beach's own funeral mass was held at Santa Rita on November 29, 1954. Her second husband, Charles Beach, was remembered with memorial services at the Shrine upon his death 13 years later on November 26, 1967.

I by no means claim the final word on the Shrine of Santa Rita, because history has as much to do with the present as it has to do with the past. What we choose to do with what we know about the past — preserve it, cherish it, or ignore it — establishes a chronicle for the future. If this record is left blank, we are responsible, because we have an enormous obligation to present and forthcoming generations to maintain and understand our past.

The pieces of this story were scattered in hidden repositories — many forgotten or not easily accessible. Death has silenced many who may have helped in the telling; but we are not too late, for enough evidence exists to assert the truth and delight in the sustainment of a small fraction of our history. Jane Herman, T. W. Kramer, John Kramer, and Virgil Johnson, all of whom knew Mrs. Beach when she lived in Vail, were most generous of their time and memories in helping me reconstruct the history of the Shrine. Dan Brosnan, archivist for the Diocese of Tucson, devoted much time and patience in guiding my search for information in the archives. Many other friends have also helped me with stories and possible leads, and to those I acknowledge my deepest gratitude.

History is still in the making in the very active parish of Santa Rita today, and this document is dedicated to all the people, the true spirit of the Church, who have made and still make the Shrine a peaceful link to our past. Santa Rita is a testimonial that whispered prayers are heard and answered from even isolated corners of the desert.

I am Ann Pearson (formerly Grigsby) and as part of the Shrine's 85th anniversary celebration, I updated this small history. I hope you enjoy it.

Ann M. Pearson
March 2020, Pasadena, Texas

Chapter One: The Inspiration

The Japanese doctor for whom the Shrine was built was
Jokichi Takamine. Born in Kanazawa, on the western
coast of Japan, on November 3, 1854, Takamine led an
active life in pursuit of knowledge and progress. He
travelled throughout the Far East, Europe, and the
United States, accumulated a vast fortune, and earned
respect and recognition from both eminent scientists
and humble farmers around the world.

As the eldest son born into a prominent family of physicians, Takamine was educated well in anticipation of his future role in the family medical profession. While still a young boy, he studied in Nagasaki and Kyoto, cities hundreds of miles from his home, and then was chosen to attend medical school in Osaka. In 1872, Takamine went to Tokyo and entered the College of Science and Engineering in the Imperial University of Tokyo recently established by the Japanese government. According to Seiichi Iwao in the *Biographical Dictionary of Japanese History*, Takamine also completed the applied chemistry course from the College of Public Works in Tokyo.

When he graduated in 1879, Takamine was one of 12 advanced students chosen by the government to receive further schooling in Great Britain. By this time, Takamine was turning away from the idea of practicing medicine and focused his attention on chemical research. He would later utilize his early medical training and education in his pharmaceutical experiments. According to his biographer Kawakami, Takamine studied chemistry in Glasgow, Scotland, at both Glasgow University and at Anderson College. All of Takamine's education and travel expenses were paid for by the government of Japan.

After three years of study in Great Britain, Takamine returned to Tokyo in 1883 and took a government position in the Japanese Department of Agriculture and Commerce. He would soon leave Japan again though, when in 1884, the Japanese government sent Takamine as a representative to an International Exposition in New Orleans, Louisiana. While in the United States, Takamine continued to travel to learn more about chemical fertilizers, knowledge he would put to profitable advantage upon returning to Japan. The 1884 New Orleans World's Exposition and Cotton Centennial was promoted as a major international event — the Liberty Bell was sent from Philadelphia to mark the auspicious occasion — even though the fair was ultimately not a financial success.

While the exposition may have been a commercial failure, it was in New Orleans that Takamine first encountered Caroline Hitch, the 18-year-old eldest daughter of Mary and Ebenezer Hitch. Caroline was born in Fairhaven, Massachusetts, on August 5, 1866, and led a rather typical nineteenth-century life until she met Jokichi Takamine while he supervised the Japanese exhibit at the exposition.

De Mille recounts that Caroline's mother, Mary Beatrice Field Hitch, was an enterprising Southern woman who had no intention of allowing an inconvenient lack of material wealth to interfere in either her ambitions for a respectable position in New Orleans society for herself or in the attainment of suitable marriages for her five surviving daughters of the thirteen children she bore her husband Ebenezer. Accordingly, just before the World's Exposition opened in New Orleans, Mrs. Hitch moved into a commodious, but dilapidated mansion in the then-unfashionable French Quarter and refurbished the living areas in readiness for exposition visitors. Ordinary boarders were not considered; Mrs. Hitch notified the Chamber of Commerce that she would accommodate the Japanese delegation. This plan must have been convenient, or Mrs. Hitch was a formidable persuader, because an invitation was sent to the Japanese delegation and arrangements were made that housed Takamine and Tamari, another Japanese scientist, under the Hitch roof during the year-long exposition.

Takamine left New Orleans in 1885 with phosphate samples from South Carolina for his agricultural experiments and with an official marriage engagement to Caroline Hitch. Many biographical sketches erroneously record the Takamine/Hitch wedding as taking place in 1885, but the actual ceremony did not occur until Takamine returned to New Orleans from Japan. He travelled to the United States two years later to procure more fertilizer machinery and to marry Caroline on August 10, 1887. The next day, the New Orleans *Daily Picayune* described the event as "A Brilliant Wedding." The guests gathered in the Hitch residence which was decorated with the traditional American wedding symbols of roses and bells while the bride wore a white dress embroidered with chrysanthemums, a gift of friendship designed and made in Japan, and walked under festive Japanese lanterns on the veranda. Soon after the wedding, the couple left for Washington, DC, where Takamine conducted business with the patent office. Takamine introduced his wife, now a Japanese imperial subject by marriage, to the Japanese Embassy. Their honeymoon included a trip to South Carolina to collect more phosphates to take back to Japan, and a typical tourist stop at Niagara Falls before heading to San Francisco to board the steamer across the ocean. By November of that year, the newlyweds were back in Tokyo.

From 1887 to 1890 the Takamines lived in Japan where Takamine had been appointed as Chief of the Division of Chemistry in the Department of Agriculture and Commerce. He later became the chief of the patent bureau also. Takamine experimented with ideas he had gathered from the New Orleans exposition and from his other travels abroad. Despite skepticism from some government officials, Takamine's successful experimentation with chemical fertilizers prompted Japanese industrial leaders to organize the Tokyo Artificial Fertilizer Company, dependent on Takamine's chemical expertise. Takamine left government service and managed the fertilizer company for three years while he continued to experiment with various chemicals unrelated to the fertilizer industry. Meanwhile, Caroline learned to cope with the pressures of being one of very few Anglo women in Japan at the time and attempted to accept her position in a marriage with a highly goal-oriented and inquisitive man. The transition from vivacious belle to submissive wife in a time when that designation was rarely questioned could not have been an easy one.

In the United States, Caroline's mother, Mary Beatrice, was instrumental in marketing her brilliant son-in-law and his scientific discoveries to the American business world while he was in Japan. De Mille explains that Mary Beatrice decided to "form a company for the manufacture of whatever Jokichi held patents for" (165). De Mille notes that with characteristic perseverance, Mary Beatrice established a corporation, bought and sold stocks, and even hawked her jewelry to support and to promote her Japanese relation in the United States. Harboring grand schemes, the Hitches cabled to Tokyo that Chicago whiskey manufacturers were interested in one of Takamine's non-fertilizer experiments.

Consequently, in 1890, Takamine was invited to demonstrate one of his scientific discoveries in Chicago. Takamine had formulated a new type of diastase, an enzyme essential in the distilling of alcohol. Simply put, diastase converts starch into sugar. Before Takamine's discovery, malt diastase made from barley was the only option for this step in the procedure for distilling alcohol. The six-month growing period required to produce the barley, and the six-day germination period needed to form malt diastase from grain was condensed by Takamine to 48 hours. This potential boon to the distillery industry is what attracted the whiskey moguls to Takamine's seemingly obscure experiments in Japan.

Abandoning the social standing of a successful and respected businessman Takamine had established in Japan, Jokichi and Caroline again crossed the Pacific Ocean bound for Seattle. By this time, the couple had two young sons, Jokichi, Jr., born August 28, 1888, and Ebenezer Takashi, born August 31, 1889.

After a successful demonstration of his new brand of diastase in Chicago, Takamine was invited to Peoria, Illinois, to repeat the diastase demonstration for Joseph Greenhut, president of the Woolner's Brothers distilling plant, the "largest whiskey trust in America at the time" (Kawakami 28). The Takamines lived in a large home, which is still standing at 2111 N. Jefferson in Peoria from 1891 to 1896 while Takamine continued his experiments. According to L. Sidney Eslinger, Peoria historian, Caroline joined the Peoria Women's Club from 1892-1896 and served on the Education Committee. For one meeting Caroline presented a program to the club on "Life in Japan."

American life seems to have settled into active domesticity for the young Takamine family; however, eventually, disgruntled malt manufacturers took notice of Takamine's successful distillery experiments. Fearing for their own livelihood, the various workers who had an interest in the production of the malt traditionally used for alcohol distillation launched a propaganda and intimidation campaign to silence Takamine and his discoveries. The distillery in which Takamine worked was burned to the ground, evidently the result of arsonists, and in 1894 the directors of the company succumbed to the pressure of the agitators by dissolving the corporation. This act signaled the virtual end of Takamine's future in the whiskey business.

Despite his brief residence in Illinois, Peorians like to remember that Takamine's connection to the beautiful cherry trees in Washington, DC, began in this state. According to Melanie Choukas-Bradley in *City of Trees*: "The world-famous Japanese cherry trees encircling the Tidal Basin in Washington's West Potomac Park were a gift to the American people from the city of Tokyo. They are probably the world's greatest living symbol of friendship between two nations" (52).

In an April 10, 1943, news clipping of "news about town" in the *Peoria Journal Transcript*, Charles B. Smith reports that around 1910 when William Howard Taft was president of the United States, Takamine had been able to interest Mrs. Helen Taft in Japanese cherry trees. Mrs. Taft was a sister of William A. Herron, a prominent Peoria banker. In 1909, Takamine supposedly used his influence in Japan to have the Japanese government send 2,000 cherry trees to be planted on the banks of the Potomac River in the nation's capital. Choukas-Bradley indicates that these first trees "proved to be infected with insect pests and plant diseases" (52). Consequently, this shipment of trees could not be accepted by the Department of Agriculture, and was burned, but Takamine continued to work toward realizing this highly visible symbol of Japanese/American friendship. Ultimately, in 1912, the mayor of Tokyo, Yukio Ozaki, "simply ordered that special precautions be taken to insure a healthy second shipment of trees" (Choukas-Bradley 52). Mrs. Taft and Viscountess Iwa Chinda, the wife of the Japanese ambassador to the United States, planted the first two cherry trees. Takamine's role in this historic event is not officially recorded; it is repeated often though in rumors, and the Peoria connection is certainly plausible considering Takamine's influence and his vast connections in both Japan and the United States.

To begin yet again, Takamine moved from Peoria in 1896 first to Chicago and then to New York where the scientist continued to experiment. During this time, Takamine brought several young Japanese scientists to the United States to assist him in his research. Takamine, the respected descendent of prominent Japanese physicians, now turned his attention to medical research. Takamine himself suffered from a painful and recurrent liver ailment, for which he had undergone surgery in 1894 by Chicago surgeons, Dr. Henrotin and Dr. Malcolm L. Harris. Perhaps with pain and suffering on his mind, Takamine hoped to develop a form of diastase to relieve indigestion. The resulting product he named Taka-Diastase. The pharmaceutical company Parke-Davis of Detroit agreed to manufacture and sell Taka-Diastase, taking out a joint patent with Takamine. They also allowed Takamine a relatively generous stipend of $300 for continued research, which allowed him to remain in his laboratories and experiment.

In 1897, the Takamine family moved both home and laboratory to New York. At his basement laboratory on East 103rd Street, Takamine worked with Keizo Wooyenaka to conduct what would prove to be the most important experiments of Takamine's professional career. In Peoria, Takamine had begun experimenting with the adrenal glands of sheep from the nearby stockyards. The end results of these malodorous and filthy experiments with bloody glands from recently slaughtered animals proved elusive. Nonetheless, despite the interruption of moving into new laboratories in New York, Takamine continued to search for the active principle in the suprarenal gland. Reports vary as to Takamine's actual participation in these experiments. De Mille acknowledges complaints made by Wooyenaka's daughter that her father made the true discovery of adrenaline, while Takamine was merely a figurehead chemist. These claims are made despite the documentation in which Takamine solely obtained a United States patent for the formula. Scientist J. J. Abel at Johns Hopkins is also credited with isolating this chemical property, but Takamine had filed for a patent for the same formula ten days earlier.

In 1901, Takamine, along with Wooyenaka, announced his ability to isolate the active principle of the suprarenal gland at a medical convention at Johns Hopkins University. At this time Takamine formally recognized the part that Wooyenaka had contributed to the medical discovery, but did not deny his own accomplishment.

Takamine earned both material wealth and international prestige because of his medical research. With his new fame, Takamine was able to continue his efforts to introduce new products and manufacturing techniques to Japan and the United States. He was also able to expand the Takamine Laboratory facilities in Clifton, New Jersey, and to increase his staff of Japanese and American chemical researchers for further experimentation. Kawakami records the numerous honors and awards Takamine received for his contributions to science and medicine. In 1899 the Imperial University in Tokyo awarded Takamine the honorary degree of Doctor of Chemical Engineering and in 1906 the title of Doctor of Pharmacy. In 1912, Takamine received a medal from the Imperial Academy of Science in Japan for the discovery of Adrenalin, and in 1913, he was made a member of the Imperial Academy. The Japanese government joined with the Japanese academic community in honoring Takamine as a favorite son. In 1915, the Emperor of Japan decorated Takamine with a Fourth Class Order of the Rising Sun, and shortly before his death in 1922 Takamine was given the Senior Degree of the Fourth

Rank (Sho Shii) and the Third Merit (Kun Santo).

According to *Who Was Who, 1916-1928,* Takamine was also a Fellow of the Chemical Society and a Member of the Chemical Industry in England; and he was likewise a member of the American Chemical Society, the Institute of Chemical Engineers, and the Electro-Chemical Society in the United States. According to William W. Scott in *History of Passaic and Its Environs,* Takamine was also:

> President of the Takamine Ferment Company of Chicago, Illinois, the Takamine International Ferment Company and the Takamine Ferment Company of New York. He was also a member of the firm of Takamine & Darby….He was president of the firm of Sankyo & Company, Limited, the largest manufactures of chemicals and pharmaceuticals in Japan…[and] was vice-president of the Asia Aluminum Company of New York and Tokyo. (372)

Along with his many awards, degrees, and positions, Takamine was respected and renown by many Japanese Americans as a type of unofficial ambassador between the two diverse countries. In 1905, he organized and initiated a social club for Japanese Americans in New York that continues today as the Nippon Club. Takamine founded the Nippon Club so Japanese Americans with limited incomes would be able to entertain their American friends and business associates in an appropriate setting. Understanding the importance of being able to reciprocate a host's hospitality, Takamine served as the club's president until his death in 1922. Takamine also contributed to the formation of the Japan Society and the Japanese Association of New York, which replaced previous mutual aid groups. Both of these groups were formed with the intent of fostering and enriching personal contact and mutual respect between Japanese immigrants and American citizens. This early concern with peaceful relations proved very beneficial when anti-Japanese agitation began before World War I and escalated during World War II.

In his on-going quest to juxtapose his Japanese origins to his American lifestyle, Takamine maintained a showpiece home in New York at 334 Riverside Drive designed to combine the greatest art and architecture of both East and West. The five-story home was originally planned to display a different time period in Japanese history on each floor. Takamine hoped to present the evolution of Japanese art and decoration in his residence. This initial plan proved too ambitious for a building that must also serve as a comfortable home, so the design was modified. Ultimately, only the first and second floors were decorated with Japanese paintings and designs. The artistic designs within the mansion were carefully chosen to represent only work that was the purest Japanese art, and not art influenced by outside schools of design. According to Kawakami, the Takamines hosted several important receptions in the Riverside mansion, inviting political dignitaries and New York socialites. Shortly before Takamine's death in 1922, Kawakami reports, the house was sold; unfortunately, in 1927, the mansion was destroyed beyond repair by fire.

In addition to this mansion in the city, the Takamines lived at Sho-Fu-Den, the estate complete with Japanese gardens, that Agnes de Mille remembers from her childhood summers in Merriewold, New York. The house, out buildings, and garden statues came from the 1904 Louisiana Purchase International Exposition held in St. Louis between December 1, 1904 and April 30, 1905. As part of an enormous display, the commissioners representing the Imperial government of Japan had constructed a Japanese landscape garden that proved to be a popular attraction. According to Mark Bennitt in *History of the Louisiana Purchase Exposition*, "Japan spared neither effort nor expense to make the most comprehensive display of her products and resources ever sent to an exposition from an Oriental country. The Government of Japan appropriated $400,000 and Formosan Government $50,000 for the exhibit" (372).

The two buildings Takamine eventually converted into a summer home in Merriewold were originally a reception hall and a business office for the Japanese exposition commission. All of the materials for the buildings, including the large stone lanterns and ornamental statues, had been finished in Japan and shipped to St. Louis ready to be re-assembled. The finished display was impressive: "Over 282, 455 square feet of space were occupied by Japan" (Bennitt 303). The Japanese plants and trees created an authentic Japanese setting which obviously appealed to Takamine's aesthetic tastes. He asked the Japanese commission for permission to remove the entire display to land he had purchased outside New York City, and the commission agreed to this proposal. Consequently, the buildings and stone fixtures were again dismantled and shipped to the forests of Merriewold, New York, and reassembled as an elegant and unique country mansion. The Imperial government recognized the potential diplomatic opportunities such a home would provide as an example of gracious Japanese hospitality, and subsequently, the Takamines did extensive entertaining at their summer home. Takamine named the estate Sho-Fu-Den, and spent many summers supervising the work in the 25-acre Japanese garden with Caroline as their children grew into adulthood.

It was at Sho-Fu-Den that the Takamines entertained Japanese royalty; in 1907 Prince and Princess Kuni visited the United States on their way from Europe back to Japan. Princess Kuni was pregnant at the time with Princess Nagako Kuniyoshi who later married Emperor Hirohito inside the Japanese Imperial Palace on January 24, 1924. De Mille records the exhausting formality of this visit on Caroline who spoke very little Japanese, but was expected to play the role of accomplished hostess to the royal couple (124). The Prince and Princess had to be treated according to the strict dictates of Japanese protocol, which left little room for casual American friendliness. The trip seems to have passed well enough though, and the small community of Merriewold had yet another Takamine story to tell.

Today, renovations are planned to preserve Sho-Fu-Den as a monument to a by-gone era. According to an article translated from the Japanese newspaper *The Yomiuri America* on March 25, 1994, the plans to restore Sho-Fu-Den are well underway through the work of the Japanese Heritage Foundation, Inc. of New York. Of the original 2,000 acres Takamine owned at the turn of the century, only about 100 acres remain as the land of the Japanese-styled estate. After Takamine's death in 1922, Caroline sold the estate to John Moody, a friend of the Takamines for years who founded Moody's Investor's Service in New York. This family owned the property and buildings until the 1940s. In 1945, Melvin Osborne purchased the estate. In 1986, Yoshitaka Ikeda, Chief Executive Officer of the Japanese Heritage Foundation purchased the estate with support from volunteers dedicated to the historical preservation of the site. According to *The Yomiuri America*, while many different businesses and groups had been considered to provide financial support for the historic landmark, Ikeda "hoped to keep Sho-Fu-Den as a cultural asset to be open to the public, and tried to find ways to honor the late Dr. Takamine's wishes to use it for cultural exchange and improvement of the Japan-U.S. friendship."

Jokichi Takamine died in New York's Lenox Hill Hospital, July 22, 1922, finally succumbing to his recurrent liver problem. The *New York Times* reported on July 15, 1922:

Dr. Jokichi Takamine, one of Japan's foremost chemists, is critically ill of a complicated kidney disease….He has been in failing health for a long time, but apparently was on the road to recovery when a relapse set in last December. In June his condition necessitated his removal to the hospital from his country home in Merriewold, NY. (9:6)

When he died, Takamine was 68 years old; he and Caroline had been married for nearly 35 years. During his last illness, knowing he would soon die, Jokichi Takamine converted to Catholicism. An article in the *New York Times* only a few days after Takamine's death claims that Takamine had joined the Catholic church six weeks before his death; the *Times* headline reads: "Takamine Buried With Catholic Rite: Noted Japanese Chemist Renounced Buddhism, Religion of His Birth Only 6 Weeks Ago." The article notes Fr. William B. Martin, the acting rector of St. Patrick's Cathedral about Takamine's conversion. Fr. Martin claims, "Takamine had been delving into the philosophies of different religions," and that Takamine desired spiritual support. Martin continues: "Of all the religions he studied, Dr. Takamine said Catholicism supplied this need the best because it was a religion of authority and revelation." Takamine received the sacraments of conversion by the Right Rev. Thomas J. Kernan of the St. Nicholas Church of Passaic, New Jersey. The account de Mille records suggests that Takamine desperately grasped on to his wife's religion in a last-ditch effort at recovery. According to de Mille, Takamine was persuaded to adopt this dramatic religious change by one of the nurses attending him at Lenox Hill who was a Roman Catholic, and he was certainly influenced by his wife Caroline who had converted several years earlier. Regardless of the exact timing, this late religious conversion thrilled Caroline, but devastated many of Takamine's friends and family.

Despite disapproval from Takamine's acquaintances, Caroline disregarded her husband's preference for cremation after his death and organized full Catholic rites for his funeral. In his will, Takamine had requested that his body either be dissected for medical research or be cremated and the ashes buried partly in the United States and partly in Japan. Since Vatican II in 1962-1963, the Catholic church's stance strictly forbidding cremation has been altered to allow for this alternative preparation after death; however, in 1922, the Church forbade cremation because it hastened the natural process of the body's return to dust. Caroline was convinced her husband was unaware cremation was against Roman Catholic doctrine, and since he had prepared his will and last testament before his religious conversion, she felt compelled to take responsibility for his final arrangements. Dr. Malcolm L. Harris, who had operated on Takamine years before, was the Chicago surgeon Takamine specified as the person to undertake the dissection for research. Dr. Harris reported to the Takamine family that "no great benefit to science" would be made through the dissection of Takamine's body. Consequently, Caroline adamantly insisted to the *New York Times* on August 4, 1922: "I am sure that Dr. Takamine did not know of the prohibition of cremation by the Catholic Church, and if he were alive now he would certainly alter the will in this respect."

The Nippon Club honored its founder with a memorial service in which Takamine lay in state on Monday, July 24, 1922. More than three hundred floral arrangements, sent by both prominent Japanese and American friends and by anonymous patients who had benefitted from Takamine's medical research, surrounded his coffin. On his body an American and a Japanese flag were crossed to represent his untiring efforts to establish friendly relations between the two countries he so esteemed. Several hundred mourners attended the services with others arriving to pay their respects throughout the evening. A special funeral mass conducted by Monsignor Kernan and Fr. Martin was celebrated at St. Patrick's Cathedral in New York on the morning of Tuesday, July 25, 1922. Takamine was buried in a newly constructed family mausoleum at Woodlawn Cemetery.

In his will, Takamine bequeathed one-third of all he owned to his wife, Caroline. He left one-sixth of the entire estate each to his sons, Jokichi and Eben, and to their wives. In addition to these family legacies, Takamine left bequests to many employees in the laboratories. His public contributions included Y50,000 to the Institute of Tokyo for chemical research, and Y25,000 to the Imperial Academy of Science, also in Tokyo.

Chapter Two: The Dream

When Jokichi Takamine died in 1922, Caroline was 56 years old and a wealthy widow, but lonely and alone. She certainly had family, but they all had personal concerns aside from Caroline's. Her grown sons had lives of their own by this time. Jokichi Jr. had attended the Sheffield Scientific School at Yale University, graduating with the degree of PhB in 1913, after which he enrolled in graduate studies in chemistry at the Pasteur Institute in Paris, France, as well as at the University of Freiburg, Germany. On June 4, 1917, Jokichi married Isabelle Hilde Petrie; the couple had two children, Caroline, born May 20, 1923, and Jokichi Takamine III, born February 6, 1924. From his father's death in 1922, Jokichi, Jr. served as President of Takamine Laboratory, Inc. in Clifton, New Jersey. Jokichi Takamine, Jr., died on February 22, 1930, in New York City. His Yale obituary concludes that Jokichi died "due to a fractured skull resulting from an accident" (298). De Mille suggests that he committed suicide by throwing himself out of a window at Manhattan's Roosevelt Hotel, although Caroline would never acknowledge this tragic possibility. He is also buried in the family mausoleum at Woodlawn Cemetery in New York.

Likewise, Eben attended Yale and roomed with his older brother, but did not graduate from the university. Eben married Ethel Johnson on September 29, 1915, but the couple divorced soon after his father's death in 1922. Eben later married Catherine McMahon and lived in Passaic, New Jersey, where he served in the family business concerns in various positions, including his role as the President of Takamine Laboratories in Clifton, upon his brother's death to his own, from 1930-1953. Shortly before his death, Eben Takamine became a United States citizen on March 20, 1953. He died only a few months later in Passaic, New Jersey, on August 28, 1953, from a stroke at the age of 63. Eben's wife Catherine made generous contributions to the Shrine of Santa Rita during her lifetime as a memorial to her husband's family.

It was Eben who introduced Caroline to Arizona and to Charles P. Beach, the Vail ranch hand with whom Eben was staying in the 1920s. The true story of Charles Beach is difficult to reconstruct; he must have had some wealth before he met Caroline, because he attended the University of Arizona in Tucson as a gentleman scholar with plenty of time to spare and was connected with Vail ranching in some way. Neither of these pursuits were open to penniless drifters early in this century. Nonetheless, rumors persist that prior to meeting Caroline, Charlie Beach, as he is remembered by those people who knew him, was dirt poor and doing odd jobs for ranchers who were indeed wealthy. This storyline suggests that Beach's greatest financial success came with his marriage to the wealthy widow Caroline Takamine. After their 1926 marriage, they constructed a large ranch house outside Vail.

Caroline visited her son and his friend in Arizona and remained to marry Charles Beach on August 16, 1926, in Tucson at St. Augustine's Cathedral. The 23-year difference in their ages seemed not to matter to either of them; in fact, numbers were completely relative since on their marriage license the not-quite 37 year-old Beach recorded his age as 39 and his 60 year-old bride admitted to 46. The legal document was duly signed by the couple, witnessed by Fr. Peter Timmermans, the rector at St. Augustine's, who later became the Right Reverend Monsignor Timmermans, Vicar General of the Diocese of Tucson; the document was then finally sealed and recorded by the now forgotten Pima County clerk, L. V. Clawson. Thus, the Beaches, young at heart, retired to the seclusion of their large Vail cattle ranch, which Caroline romantically dubbed, *El Rancho de los Ocotillos.*

Charles Pablo Beach was born September 14, 1889, in Kansas. His family moved to Colton, California, in the early 1900s. In 1912 he graduated from Los Angeles High School. He then attended the University of Arizona in Tucson from 1913 to 1916 and studied "mining and cattle" in the department of Agriculture. He played baseball as the team captain, and participated in basketball and football; he was on the Junior Play cast; and he was a member of the Sigma Pi Alpha fraternity. He was also a Cadet 1st Lieutenant in Company B of the student military squad, and later served in the United States Army in WWI.

Beach served as Republican member of the state fish and game commission from 1933-1951. In this role, Beach took an active part in preserving the valuable desert in and near Vail. On January 22, 1940, University of Arizona agriculture specialists led a range tour over the Beach ranch and the Santa Rita range reserve to demonstrate results of experimental work. In addition to this public position connected to wildlife and ranching, Beach was also active in mining claims in the Twin Buttes area.

In the early 1930s, Charlie and Caroline Beach planned and executed the construction of a Catholic church in Vail for the benefit of the poor Mexican families who worked on the ranches and for the Southern Pacific Railroad, but who did not have a priest to administer the sacraments and serve their other spiritual needs. The chapel would be erected as a memorial to the Takamine family, especially Caroline's first husband, Jokichi Takamine.

Charlie Beach engineered the landscaping of the church grounds to present the image that the Shrine grew up out of the surrounding desert. The illusion served a partly aesthetic and partly utilitarian purpose. The simple lines of the buildings do blend into the desert beautifully, but until 1967, the church grounds only received water from cisterns that collected the sparse rain water and occasional water tanks on the trains. So precious little water would be accessible for any reason, especially not for maintaining non-native plants and landscaping. Consequently, four large saguaros stood as silent desert guardians before the doors of the chapel, and other cacti served for decoration on the grounds. Charlie Beach continued to take an active interest in the Shrine until he died. In 1963 he made a generous contribution to the New Water Well fund at the church, and evidently visited the Shrine often to see how the grounds were kept up, making suggestions for changes and improvements. His 1965 Christmas card, now in the Arizona Historical Society Archives, depicted a watercolor sketch of the Shrine.

The architect the Beaches engaged to build the church was HDR Figge, who "planned the mission so it would carry some of the feeling of a rural Mexican church" (Cosulich). D. Burr DuBois modified Figge's plans and incorporated lighting fixtures and the interior features of the chapel. John D. Steffens was the actual construction manager. Painting was finished by Walter Ross, and W. L. Jones did the iron work. The small interior seats about 115 worshipers and has a central nave that is only 36 feet long and 27 feet wide.

The many stained-glass windows that grace Santa Rita were ones Caroline salvaged from the First Methodist Church in Tucson, which was moving to more commodious accommodations near the University of Arizona in the early 1930s, and so would no longer need the beautiful windows. In essence, Santa Rita was built around the rescued windows, and the stained glass does serve as a focal point for the church. Three round, rose windows are placed at the back entry and in the two side rooms off the altar, and each side wall contains three long, slender, and colorful windows. The large altar window diffuses the sunlight as time slowly moves across the chapel.

That the depiction of the Ten Commandments in the window directly behind the altar is a Protestant interpretation of the Old Testament dividing the commandments into the first four rules and the final six, instead of the Catholic reading emphasizing the connection between the first three statutes as distinct from the other seven, does not detract from the beauty of the image. Herself an adult convert to Catholicism, Caroline may not have realized this insignificant discrepancy; however, her past life in which she experienced and celebrated tolerance and acceptance toward difference also suggests that she may have known the window presented a differing perspective, and decided that the diversity it represented could stand as a reminder to all that despite our religious and philosophical differences, we serve one and the same God. Regardless, the tiny church in the middle of the desert was to have its beauty and the stained-glass windows were only the beginning. Caroline ensured that the finest gifts were donated to the Church, if not directly from herself, through her many wealthy and influential friends in the United States, Japan, and Europe.

The altar linens were sent by the sisters of the convent of Our Lady of Lourdes in New York, according to the report given by *Arizona Daily Star* reporter Bernice Cosulich, who attended the 1935 dedication ceremony. An original vestment in green and gold for the priests to wear during Mass was made in Japan and was sent from the Taguchi family. The original organ, which has been replaced, was a gift given by friends in Japan.

The hand-carved crucifix from Oberammergau, Bavaria, was donated to Santa Rita by Elizabeth King of Chicago. It is a replica of a crucifix that was the site of a miraculous viewing by a young boy who claims he saw the original crucifix cry real tears and bleed drops of blood as the child prayed. The original Latin missal was printed in Belgium. The missal stand was the gift of Mr. and Mrs. Nishio of New York.

The prominent green marble baptismal font was designed in Italy and was the gift of New York financial analyst John Moody, a friend Mrs. Beach knew from her days in Merriewold, New York, at Sho-Fu-Den. The small statues of St. Mary and of St. Rita located in niches at the front of the church were also both formed in Italy, and were donated to Santa Rita by Mrs. Cleaveland Putnam.

In keeping with the natural and native aspect of the chapel, the altar and tabernacle are made from stone hewn from the nearby Santa Rita Mountain Range; the altar weighs five tons. This important part of the church was donated by Mrs. Eben Takamine and her two children, Caroline's youngest son's family. Recently the church community decided to cover the rough stone surface with a marble facade, but the natural beauty of the original altar can still be seen from the rear-view. The Stations of the Cross are made from California tile. The chapel bell was a gift from Caroline's son, Eben Takamine, and was cast especially for Santa Rita.

Chapter Three: The Mission

On March 31, 1935, Charlie and Caroline Beach's dream and gift became reality for the small community of Vail. The dedication ceremony was celebrated with Tucson's first American-born bishop, Bishop Daniel J. Gercke, officiating before 600 visitors on that Sunday afternoon. Several priests from Tucson attended the ceremony, including Fr. Leo Gattes, Chaplain of St. Joseph's Academy and the Editor of the *Arizona Catholic Herald*, the official weekly newspaper of the Diocese of Tucson; Fr. Arthur Gramer, Associate Rector of St. Augustine's Cathedral; Fr. Estanislaus Caralt, Associate Pastor of Santa Cruz Church; Fr. James Davis and Fr. John Howard, Pastor and Associate Pastor of Sts. Peter and Paul Church; Fr. Jeremiah Mulcahy, recuperating at Tucson's St. Mary's Sanitorium; and Fr. J. Gordon. As a special guest of Bishop Gercke, the Most Rev. Edmund Gibbons, DD, Bishop of Albany, New York, also attended the ceremony. During the dedication, Tucson's Bishop Gercke announced:

I wish to express my deep approval and appreciation for this gift and to commend Mrs. Beach highly for what she has so thoughtfully and generously done. She has been most kind to provide for the spiritual necessities of the people around her and I hope this gift may serve as an incentive and example to others whom God has blessed with the world's goods, that they too may return some of these in gifts of charity. I hope Santa Rita in the Desert may become a sermon in stone to others and make them realize that blessings are not given them for themselves alone.

First encircling the outside walls and offering a blessing on the structure itself, Bishop Gercke dedicated the inside of the chapel to a long life of service to the residents of Vail.

Most likely the Bishop conferred a special blessing on the parishioners and guests at the conclusion of the ceremony. The festivities continued on the church grounds with an outside barbeque dinner served to the guests. The next day, the *Arizona Daily Star* recorded that "at the edge of the grounds long tables were laid on saw horses while near them several men tended the barbeque pits where two steers from the Beach ranch had been cooking slowly for hours."

The Bishop of Albany, Bishop Gibbons, was staying with Bishop Gercke at the Bishop's residence on the grounds of St. Augustine's Cathedral between March and May 1935 while Bishop Gibbons recuperated from a severe case of laryngitis. He met Charlie and Caroline Beach and kept up an active correspondence with the Beaches and Bishop Gercke for years after he returned to New York. The beauties of Arizona made a great impression on Bishop Gibbons. A little over a year after the dedication of Santa Rita's, Bishop Gibbons wrote a personal letter to Bishop Gercke noting:

> What you say of the growth of Santa Rita of the Desert, deeply interests me. Many a time I have told my clergy of that lovely little mission and the ceremony of its dedication. How can I ever forget the barbeque, especially those beans! Lest I forget, be sure to give Mr. and Mrs. Beech [sic] my kindest regards. Tell her that the little Indian bell still reminds me every day of her spiritual necessities and, as I promised her, secures for her a memento in my Mass.

 The Shrine of Santa Rita in the Desert began service as a mission. From 1935 to 1968, Franciscan priests officially assigned to San Xavier del Bac near Vail and later from the Our Mother of Sorrows parish in Tucson would come to Vail to celebrate Mass and administer the sacraments to the Catholics who lived in and near Vail.

The first priest who served Santa Rita was the Reverend Arnold Oscar, a Franciscan Father at San Xavier del Bac. He was the missionary priest at Santa Rita from 1935-1937.

The second priest in Vail was Fr. Constant Mandin, who served Santa Rita from 1937-1943. Fr. Mandin was born May 19, 1878, in Vendée, France, and studied at the Seminary of Lucan in his native Vendée. He came to the United States and was ordained in San Antonio, Texas, by Bishop John A. Forrest on March 4, 1904.

Upon his ordination, Fr. Mandin was assigned to the Church of the Sacred Heart in Prescott, Arizona, for nine years. On June 29, 1910, Fr. Mandin became a naturalized US citizen in Prescott. In 1913, Fr. Mandin was assigned to Bisbee, Arizona, where he was the founding pastor at St. Patrick's Catholic Church and served there for the next 14 years. On Sunday, March 3, 1929, Tucson's Bishop Gercke and many other diocese leaders travelled to Bisbee to congratulate Fr. Mandin on his Silver Jubilee celebration mass attended by the large Bisbee congregation and many visitors. Both the Tucson *Daily Citizen* and the Bisbee *Daily Review* reported on the special occasion. During his sermon, the bishop praised Mandin for "his zeal and love for God." The bishop also noted that "the example of his priestly life has been a source of edification to all, even to those not of our faith." The grateful congregation surprised Fr. Mandin with a $4,000 check that carried the stipulation that the money be used only for personal expenditures. The much-loved and dedicated pastor had never taken any salary for his services at St. Patrick's. He planned to spend part of his gift on a trip to his homeland of France to visit friends and family he had not seen for the 24 years he had served the Church in Arizona. From 24 April to 24 June 1929, Fr. Mandin's passport declares he did indeed visit Vendee on the munificence of his grateful parishioners.

Fr. Mandin left Bisbee for Vail in 1937 when a breakdown in his health forced him to retire from his active parish duties at St. Patrick's. The Bishop agreed that the quiet solitude of Vail would be an ideal place of retirement for Fr. Mandin. Fr. Mandin oversaw the construction of the St. Rita rectory shortly after the church was constructed. A picture of a youthful Fr. Mandin hangs in the rectory today inscribed: "In loving memory to Father Constant Mandin who built this rectory as a haven of rest and peace." Fr. Mandin died in Vail on February 3, 1943. He is buried in the special priests' section of Holy Hope Cemetery in Tucson.

Bishop Gercke announced on February 27, 1943, that the pastorate of Santa Rita in the Desert in Vail would be assumed by the Reverend George Jonaitis, who had been serving as chaplain to the Franciscan Sisters in Tucson. Fr. Jonaitis served Santa Rita as its third priest through World War II from 1943-1948. Born in 1880, Fr. Jonaitis came to the United States from Lithuania when he was 18 years old. He studied at St. Bonaventure's College in New York state and continued his education in Belgium. After attending St. Paul's Seminary in Minnesota, he was ordained a priest in Omaha, Nebraska, in 1910.

Fr. Jonaitis volunteered for service in World War I as a private in the Army and was later commissioned a first lieutenant as a chaplain, leaving the service as a major. His right arm was wounded while he was in France just before the Armistice. Upon returning to the United States after the war, Fr. Jonaitis was assigned to St. Peter's Church in Detroit, Michigan. He left this assignment to be a lecturer in Lithuania before his next assignment to St. Peter's Church in Stanton, Nebraska. Fr. Jonaitis resigned from this parish and moved to Tucson in an attempt to alleviate the pain he experienced from arthritis and problems associated with his war wound. After an active semi-retirement in the Tucson area, including his role as chaplain for St. Mary's Hospital, and chaplain for the Federal Youth Camp on Mt. Lemmon, in addition to his pastorate in Vail, Fr. Jonaitis left Arizona in 1962 for Omaha, Nebraska. On December 26, 1963, he died of an apparent heart attack at St. Vincent's Home in Omaha, a residence for elderly priests; Fr. Jonaitis was 83 years old. A pontifical requiem Mass was celebrated for Fr. Jonaitis at St. Cecilia's Cathedral in Omaha by the Most Reverend Gerald T. Bergan, Archbishop of Omaha.

Beginning in 1948, Reverend William Henry Gockel served Santa Rita for three years, his first of four separate periods as missionary priest to Santa Rita's. He later served as priest from 1953-54, 1955-1962, and in 1967. Born in Cincinnati, Ohio, April 19, 1898, Fr. Gockel was ordained June 11, 1927, in Covington, Kentucky, by Bishop Francis W. Howard, DD. Fr. Gockel was Assistant Pastor and Pastor at several parishes in Kentucky before coming to Arizona. From 1945, Fr. Gockel was on sick leave from the Diocese of Covington. He served at the Immaculate Conception Church in Douglas, Arizona, but was also forced to spend time at a sanitorium in Albuquerque, New Mexico, because of his ill health during the late 1940s. Fr. Gockel spent $600 he had inherited from a family member in Connecticut to install the Crucifixion group that now hangs in the back of the church. When it was first displayed at Santa Rita's, the group hung behind the altar and the three figures of Christ, the Virgin Mary, and John the Apostle were backed by a climbing rhododendron vine that partially covered the stained-glass window.

In September 1962, Bishop Green appointed Fr. Gockel Chaplain to Villa Maria de Guadalupe Home for the Aged in Tucson. Fr. Gockel died November 28, 1983, and is buried in the Priests' Cemetery, Seminary of St. Pius X, in Erlanger, Kentucky.

From 1951-1953 Fr. William Leaver served as pastor at Santa Rita's. Fr. Leaver was born on May 24, 1889, in Cincinnati, Ohio. He was educated in Ohio, attending Mt. St. Mary's and Mt. Washington in Cincinnati for his seminary work from 1912-1918. Fr. Leaver was ordained May 25, 1918, by Archbishop Henry Moeller in his hometown of Cincinnati. All of Fr. Leaver's assignments upon his ordination were within Ohio, including his role as Pastor of Sacred Heart Church in Milford, Ohio, for 25 years.

Fr. Leaver came to the Diocese of Tucson for his health on September 10, 1949. For the last few years of his life, Fr. Leaver was seriously ill and lived with his sister Rosemary Leaver in Tucson. He died on September 15, 1970, at the age of 81. A scripture service was held for Fr. Leaver at the Tucson Mortuary on the evening of September 18, and a funeral mass was concelebrated the next morning at St. Augustine's Cathedral in Tucson. Fr. Leaver is also buried in Tucson's Holy Hope Cemetery.

Fr. Edward Richard assumed responsibility for Santa Rita from 1954-1955 after Fr. Gockel's second assignment in 1953-1954.

In 1962 the Rev. Harold Richard Flower, from the Order of St. Benedict, became Santa Rita's assigned priest with the title of "administrator" to the Shrine. Fr. Flower was born May 11, 1890, in Ypsilanti, Michigan, but was not baptized in the Catholic Church until June 28, 1930, at Belmont Abbey in Hereford, England. He received a BA in 1912 from the University of Michigan, and an MA of Philosophy in 1920 from the University of Chicago. He attended seminary at St. Benedict's Abbey in Ft. Augustus, Scotland, from 1931-1936, and was ordained December 8, 1936, at Ft. Augustus Abbey, Scotland, by the Most Rev. George Bennett, Bishop of Aberdeen, Scotland. From 1937-1939 Fr. Flower served as the head of the Modern Languages department at the Order of St. Benedict Priory in Portsmouth, Rhode Island.

Like many other priests, Fr. Flower also came to Tucson for his declining health; he first came in the summers of 1947 and 1948, and then remained in Arizona from 1952 to his death in 1974. During his residence in Tucson, Fr. Flower served in numerous roles within the diocese. He was assistant pastor at the parishes of Sts. Peter and Paul, St. Ambrose, and St. Joseph in Tucson. From 1958-1969, Fr. Flower served as the chaplain for St. Joseph's Academy, a parochial boarding school in Tucson; and he served on Bishop Francis Green's Diocesan Commission on Ecumenical Affairs, a post-Vatican II committee established in 1965 to "insure a unified and friendly relationship with our non-Catholic brethren" according to the article in the *Arizona Register*, a Catholic regional newspaper reporting on the commission's formation. From November 1961 to December 31, 1964, Fr. Flower also undertook the responsibilities of administrator of the Shrine of Santa Rita in Vail. Fr. Flower was an active administrator for Santa Rita during his three-year period; however, because of his numerous other duties in Tucson, he did not reside at the rectory in Vail. Charles J. Murphy, the caretaker, and his wife, lived at the rectory during this period and cared for the grounds.

In consideration of his failing health, Fr. Flower requested Bishop Green relieve him of his duties in the still sparsely populated area that constituted the congregation of Santa Rita at the end of 1964. From 1969 until his final illness, Fr. Flower served Our Mother of Sorrows in various roles, culminating in his position as Associate Pastor. On June 13, 1971, Fr. Flower suffered a transitory stroke and remained hospitalized in various institutions until his death on January 9, 1974, at St. Mary's hospital in Tucson; Fr. Flower was 83 years old. A memorial Mass was celebrated at Our Mother of Sorrows in Tucson on Monday morning, January 14. Funeral services and Fr. Flower's burial took place in Portsmouth, Rhode Island.

At the end of 1964, when Fr. Flower left Santa Rita's, Bishop Green was unable to immediately fill the position of administrator for the Shrine. In a December letter, Bishop Green asked Fr. Philip Poirier, Pastor at Our Mother of Sorrows, "to take care of the few people who use those facilities."

For the year 1966-1967, Fr. Robert Rohrich, from the order of the Congregation of the Missions, served at Santa Rita's. Fr. Rohrich was born June 28, 1934, in Chicago, Illinois. He was educated in Illinois and Missouri, attending St. Mary's Seminary in Perryville, Missouri, from 1952-1957. Fr. Rohrich received a BA from St. Mary's Seminary in 1957, and an MA in History from De Paul University in 1965. He was ordained as a priest on May 28, 1961, by Cardinal Joseph Ritter in Perryville, Missouri.

In May 1967, Fr. Albert Wilson came to Santa Rita from the Society of the Divine Savior. Fr. Wilson was born on October 8, 1913, in Escanaba, Michigan. He was ordained into the Society of the Divine Savior on June 11, 1940. In August of 1943 Fr. Wilson entered the United States Army as a chaplain stationed in the Pacific, Germany, and later Korea. Fr. Wilson came to Vail after 23 years of military service, retiring in 1966 as a Lt. Col. Only a few months after arriving, Fr. Wilson oversaw a major repair project on the stained-glass windows of the church. Viewing the altar from the church, the right-hand window behind the altar originally displayed an open Bible, but was replaced with a window depicting the image of a cross and crown now in the church. Fr. Wilson died November 24, 1968, in Vail. A funeral Mass was held November 26 at the Shrine of Santa Rita. He is buried in the Salvatorian cemetery at St. Nazianz, Wisconsin.

Fr. Wilson began the Salvatorian tradition at the Shrine that continues today. Brother Edward Havlovic, SDS, archivist for the Society of the Divine Savior, explains that "in February of 1967, Rev. Philip Poirier, pastor of Mother of Sorrows parish in Tucson, read an article in the *National Catholic Reporter* about the Savatorians." That same month Fr. Poirier extended an invitation to the Superior of the Salvatorians to help in the Diocese of Tucson by sending a semi-retired Salvatorian priest to Vail. Fr. Poirier, with Bishop Green's permission and blessing, arranged to have the Salvatorians assume the responsibilities of the administration of Santa Rita's small church community.

Father James Roeske SDS

The Shrine was established as a parish in 1968. During 1968-1969, Fr. James Roeske, SDS, served at Santa Rita's. Fr. Roeske was born on May 6, 1912, in Chicago, Illinois, the eighth oldest of 18 children.

Fr. Roeske was ordained on June 6, 1950, after he completed his studies for the priesthood at the Catholic University of America in Washington, DC. Most of his official life was spent as the associate pastor of Mother of Good Counsel parish in Milwaukee, Wisconsin. Fr. Roeske spent only about a year in Vail. He died after suffering for several years from a lingering illness at St. Joseph's Hospice in Milwaukee on December 4, 1982; Fr. Roeske is buried in the Salvatorian cemetery at St. Nazianz, Wisconsin.

The year 1969 introduced to Santa Rita the church's most permanent servant in the familiar figure of Brother Camillus Becker, SDS. Brother, as he is affectionately known, maintains the extensive desert landscaping surrounding the church buildings. He assists the priests at all Masses from his honored position at the front of the church. One of ten children, many of whom have served the Church, Brother Camillus was born February 1, 1908, in Plainsville, Kansas, and made his first religious Profession of Vows on March 19, 1936. He was assigned to Jordan College in Menominee, Michigan, as the general maintenance man from 1936-1939. From 1939-1952 Brother went to Elkton, Maryland, to the Salvatorian Mission House as the Cook until he came to Vail in 1969 along with Fr. Messmer. Brother celebrated his Golden Jubilee of his religious service in 1986 and now lives a very active semi-retirement in the quiet of the desert.

From 1969-1973, Fr. Hermenegild George Messmer, also a Salvatorian, served the growing parish community in Vail. Fr. Messmer was born February 28, 1902, in Landshut-Achdorf, Germany.

Fr. Messmer studied in Germany and Austria, attending Seminary from 1926-1927 in Passau, Germany, before arriving in the United States to attend the Catholic University of America in Washington, DC, from September 1927 to June 1932. Fr. Messmer was ordained on June 9, 1931, at the Shrine of the Immaculate Conception in Washington, DC, by Thomas J. Shahan, DD. For the first nine years of his priesthood, Fr. Messmer was a seminary teacher in Wisconsin and Washington, DC. Then from July 1941 to July 1962, he served as a Missionary Pastor at Mother Mary Mission and St. Joseph Mission both in Alabama. From August 1962 to August 1968, Fr. Messmer served as Pastor at Holy Trinity Church in School Hill, a small rural parish in Wisconsin, where he was instrumental in constructing a new church building. He was next assigned for a year as the Pastor for Mother Mary Mission again in Alabama and at St. Joseph's Mission, which he founded in Huntsville. Leaving Alabama, Fr. Messmer came to Vail to serve as the Administrator of the Shrine of Santa Rita from 1969-1973. He left to return in retirement to Germany in 1974. Fr. Messmer died when he was 74 years old on October 13, 1977, in Germany.

In December 1973, Fr. Daniel Carroll, SDS, took over the administrative duties at the Shrine for several months. Born in Chicago, Illinois, on March 21, 1916, Fr. Carroll attended the Divine Savior Seminary in Lanham, Maryland, from 1940-1944. Fr. Carroll was ordained a priest on February 5, 1944, in Lanham by Bishop John McNamara. Fr. Carroll spent over 30 years in the capacity of teacher and missionary around the United States and in Columbia, South America. Before coming to Arizona, from 1964-1973, Fr. Carroll served as the Chaplain of the Irapuato Leper Dispensary and Clinic in Guanajuato, Mexico. Fr. Carroll died September 5, 2002, and is buried in St. Nazianz, Wisconsin.

Father Vincent Putzer SDS

The next Salvatorian priest to serve Santa Rita was Fr. Joseph Michael Vincent Putzer, who served in Vail from 1974-1983. Fr. Putzer was born in Oshkosh, Wisconsin, on January 2, 1913.

Fr. Putzer studied in Wisconsin and attended the seminary at Catholic University of America in Washington, DC, studying Philosophy and Theology from 1935-1941. He was ordained in Washington, DC, on June 11, 1940, at the Shrine of the Immaculate Conception. From 1941-1942, Fr. Putzer served as Assistant Pastor at Mother of Good Counsel Church in Milwaukee. For the next 11 years, Fr. Putzer was the Procurator and Teacher at the Salvatorian Seminary in St. Nazianz, Wisconsin. He would return to St. Nazianz from 1962-1965. From 1953-1956 he moved to the Jordan Seminary in Menominee, Michigan, in the same capacity. From 1956-1962 Fr. Putzer served as Superior Procurator and Teacher at Trinity College in Sioux City, Iowa. Fr. Putzer spent 1966-1967 as Chaplain at St. Francis Hospital in Grennell, Iowa, before moving to Arizona where he served as Chaplain at St. Joseph's Hospital in Tucson from 1967-1974. For the nine years Fr. Putzer resided at Santa Rita's, he enjoyed painting oil and water color pictures of the desert landscape surrounding the church in his spare time from his parish duties. Many of his finished art works still hang in the rectory and in parishioners' homes today.

It was during Fr. Putzer's administration of the parish that the social hall was added to the church property. The building itself has quite a history and was purchased by the church for $1 from the Vail Elementary School. According to *The Arizona Daily Star* reporter, Judith Ratliff, prior to this move, the building, "built in Territorial Days . . . first served as a schoolhouse at Pantano, [and] a Wells Fargo Stage station on Marsh Station Road east of Tucson. The building was moved to Vail in 1955" (2C). Fr. Putzer left Vail in 1983, and died on August 28, 1993. Fr. Putzer is buried in St. Nazianz, Wisconsin.

On August 1, 1983, Fr. Claude Raymond Klotz, SDS, came to Vail and served as administrator until March 1987. Fr. Klotz was born May 18, 1916, in Kenosha, Wisconsin.

Like many Salvatorians, Fr. Klotz attended the Divine Savior Seminary in Lanham, Maryland, and Catholic University of America in Washington, DC. Fr. Klotz was ordained in Trinity Chapel in Washington, DC, on May 29, 1943, by the Most Reverend John McNamara, Auxiliary Bishop of Baltimore. Upon his ordination, with a BA in theology from CUA, Fr. Klotz served the Salvatorian Seminary in St. Nazianz, Wisconsin, as a teacher of Latin, Greek, and History from 1943 to 1950. He would return to the Seminary from 1962-1965 as Treasurer and Teacher. In between these assignments, Fr. Klotz was Assistant Pastor for Mother of Good Counsel Parish in Milwaukee, Wisconsin, for 12 years. For the next 16 years, from 1965-1981, Fr. Klotz was Pastor at Good Shepherd Parish in Sheridan, Oregon, where a new church and rectory were built. Fr. Klotz moved to Arizona in July 1983 and stayed until March 1987; he recalls the "years at St. Rita were wonderful years." Fr. Klotz remembers the young boys sent to Vail to do public service work in lieu of serving time in juvenile detention homes. In 1985, the *Salvatorian Newsletter* reported that "the Arizona Correctional Training Center" sent the boys: "In order to keep out of jail or to pay fines adolescents in trouble with the law are assigned to put in so many hours of community work" (3). The boys cleaned up the grounds of the church. Years after this, Fr. Klotz stayed in touch with one man who first came to Santa Rita in this capacity. Fr. Klotz died June 7, 2006 and is buried at the Salvatorian Cemetery in St. Nazianz, Wisconsin.

For five months in 1987, Fr. Tulio Maya, a Salvatorian priest born in Colombia, South America, served the Catholic community of Vail. Fr. Maya was born on October 8, 1931, and was ordained in Rome on December 8, 1956, by Cardinal Alysus Massella. He studied Theology at Gregorian University in Rome, as well as in Germany, and at Loyola Marymount University in Los Angeles, California. Fr. Maya has worked as a priest and psychologist in the United States, Spain, Italy, and Columbia.

Fr. Donald (Robert) Verhagen, SDS, came to Santa Rita on September 1, 1987. Fr. Verhagen was born January 21, 1919, in Kaukauna, Wisconsin. He attended the Salvatorian Seminary for two years and the Divine Savior Seminary for two years from 1932-1936. Fr. Verhagen received a MS in Biology from Catholic University of America in 1955. He was ordained in Green Bay, Wisconsin, on May 19, 1945, by Bishop Stanislaus Bona. For seven years after his ordination, Fr. Verhagen was an Instructor at the Salvatorian Seminary in St. Nazianz, Wisconsin. After his graduate studies in Biology, Fr. Verhagen became the Principal of St. Mary's High School in Lancaster, New York, from 1955-1964 and the Principal of Marian High School in Mishawaka, Indiana, from 1964-1971. From 1971-1975 Fr. Verhagen served as Associate Pastor at St. Pius X Parish in Wauwatosa, Wisconsin. For the next ten years Fr. Verhagen was Co-Pastor at St. Mark's Parish in Phoenix, Arizona. For two years, 1985-1987, he served as associate Pastor at Queen of Peace Parish in Mesa, Arizona, before moving to Vail. He retired in 1996 and died on September 20, 2001, in Wisconsin.

Since the first printing of this history in 1996, four additional priests have served Santa Rita.

Fr. Robert Wicht, SDS, 1996-2008.

Fr. John F. Allt, born in Cambridge, Massachusetts, and grew up in Yuma, Arizona, served at Santa Rita July 2008 — January 2017.

Fr. Martin S. Martinez, born in Tucson, served at Santa Rita January 2017 — January 2020.

 Fr. Alonzo Garcia, born in Tucson, started serving Santa Rita on February 29, 2020.

While the priestly administrators to Vail's Shrine of Santa Rita have changed with the passing of time, each holy servant has left an indelible mark on the rich fabric of the church. Many priests were instrumental in preserving the physical beauty of Santa Rita's. Others established far-reaching parish organizations that still serve the Catholic community in Vail. Their experiences from within other parishes in the Diocese of Tucson and from around the world, through the devastation of world wars, and through the radical changes both in the modern Church and in modern social history, all contribute to influence the tiny chapel in rural Arizona. The portals of the church enclose the secrets of its vibrant history, but the walls simultaneously whisper intriguing hints linking us to the past. The prayers of those for whom the early history of the church is remembered — the Beaches, the Takamines, Fr. Mandin — are gently mingled with our own no-less-significant prayers to affect a triumphant chorus of whispered prayers from the desert fondly recalling our past as we eagerly anticipate our future.

www.ingramcontent.com/pod-product-compliance
Lightning Source LLC
Chambersburg PA
CBHW031217160726
47992CB00006B/2771